War Children

Fiona Macdonald

Great Clarendon Street, Oxford OX2 6DP

Oxford University Press is a department of the University of Oxford.
It furthers the University's objective of excellence in research, scholarship,
and education by publishing worldwide in

Oxford New York

Auckland Cape Town Dar es Salaam Hong Kong Karachi
Kuala Lumpur Madrid Melbourne Mexico City Nairobi
New Delhi Shanghai Taipei Toronto

With offices in

Argentina Austria Brazil Chile Czech Republic France Greece
Guatemala Hungary Italy Japan Poland Portugal Singapore
South Korea Switzerland Thailand Turkey Ukraine Vietnam

Oxford is a registered trade mark of Oxford University Press
in the UK and in certain other countries

First published 2005

British Library Cataloguing in Publication Data

Data available

ISBN-13: 978-0-19-919857-3
ISBN-10: 0-19-919857-8

1 3 5 7 9 10 8 6 4 2

Printed in China by Imago

Acknowledgements

The publisher would like to thank the following for permission to reproduce photographs:
p1t Hulton-Deutsch Collection/Corbis UK Ltd., p1c AKG – Images, p1b Bettmann/Corbis UK Ltd.; p4 Bettmann/Corbis UK Ltd.; p5l Corbis UK Ltd., p5r Bettmann/Corbis UK Ltd.; p6t Bettmann/Corbis UK Ltd., p6b Hulton-Deutsch Collection/Corbis UK Ltd.; p7t Hulton-Deutsch Collection/Corbis UK Ltd., p7b Robert Opie Collection; p8t TopFoto, p8b Hulton-Deutsch Collection/Corbis UK Ltd.; p9 Thom Lang/Corbis UK Ltd.; p10l Hulton-Deutsch Collection/Corbis UK Ltd., p10r AKG - Images; p11t Hulton-Deutsch Collection/Corbis UK Ltd., p11b AKG – Images; p12t Bettmann/Corbis UK Ltd., p12b Hulton-Deutsch Collection/Corbis UK Ltd.; p13 AKG – Images; p14 Austrian Archives/Corbis UK Ltd.; p15 AKG – Images; p16t Ullstein/AKG – Images, p16b Bettmann/Corbis UK Ltd.; p18l&r Hulton-Deutsch Collection/Corbis UK Ltd.; p19t Hulton-Deutsch Collection/Corbis UK Ltd., p19b Corbis UK Ltd.; p20 Hulton-Deutsch Collection/Corbis UK Ltd.; p21t Corbis UK Ltd., p21b Mme. Rogalle/ariege.com; p22t TopFoto, p22b Hulton-Deutsch Collection/Corbis UK Ltd.; p23 Bettmann/Corbis UK Ltd.

Cover photo: Arthur Rothstein/Corbis UK Ltd.

Illustrations by Oxford Designers and Illustrators

Design by Andy Wilson

Contents

Introduction

From 1939 to 1945, the world fought a terrible war. It was the most destructive war there had ever been. Battleships were sunk, tanks were blown up, and planes were shot down. Cities were flattened by bombs: homes, shops and schools were destroyed. Almost 60 million men, women and children died. Millions more nearly starved to death, or suffered horrible injuries.

Who fought in the War?

- Britain and the **Allies**
- Germany and the **Axis Powers**
- The **USSR**

Soldiers, sailors and aircrew all fought bravely. One in five did not survive.

Why did the war begin?

From 1933, Germany was ruled by the **Nazi** political party. The Nazis thought Germans were the 'master race', and wanted to rule the world. Britain and its Allies fought to stop them.

Six years of war

1938 — 1939 — 1940 — 1941 — 1942

1939 Germany invades Poland. Britain and the Allies declare war.

1940 Germany occupies (takes over) most of Europe.

1941 Germany invades USSR. Japan attacks US ships, and as a result, US joins Allies.

1942 Japan conquers South-East Asia.

German Nazi leader Adolf Hitler giving a Nazi salute.

British leader Winston Churchill making a 'V for Victory' sign.

The World at War

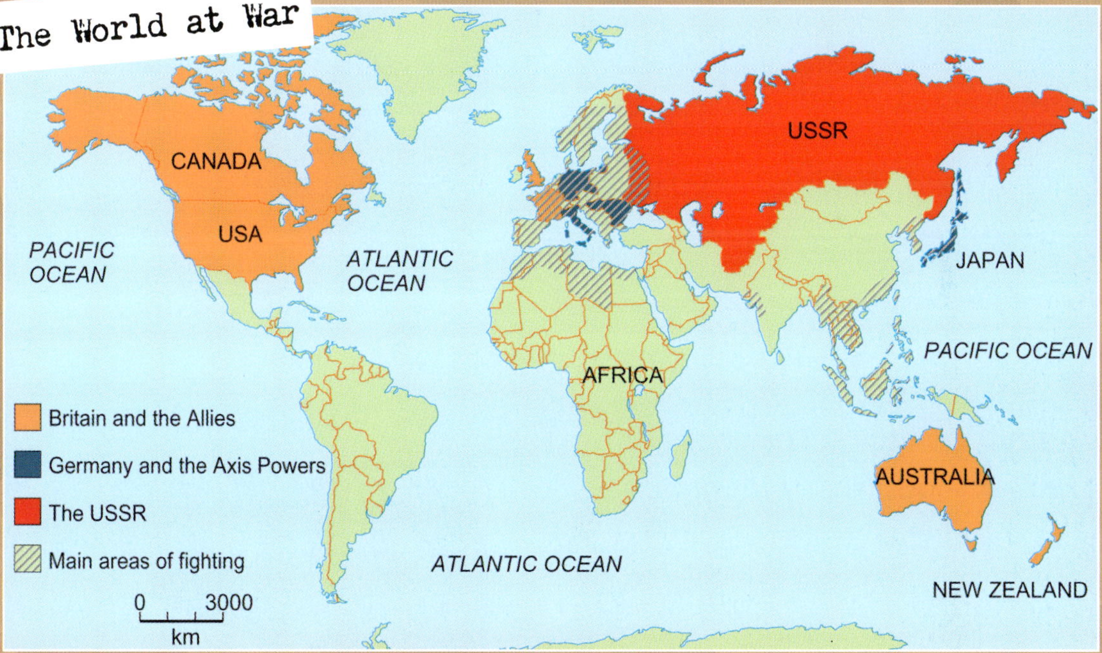

CANADA
USA
PACIFIC OCEAN
ATLANTIC OCEAN
USSR
JAPAN
PACIFIC OCEAN
AFRICA
AUSTRALIA
ATLANTIC OCEAN
NEW ZEALAND

Britain and the Allies
Germany and the Axis Powers
The USSR
Main areas of fighting

0 3000
km

1943 Allies defeat Germans in North Africa and Italy.

1944 USSR defeats German invaders. Allies attack Germans in France; USSR invades Germany.

1945 Allies invade Germany, Hitler kills himself. Germany surrenders.

USA drops first atom bombs on Japan.

1943 1944 1945 1946

Preparing for War

Because of the growing threat of the Nazis in Germany in the late 1930s, other nations feared there might soon be war. In Britain, the government bought weapons, built warships and made plans to protect people. They floated huge **barrage balloons** in the sky, to stop German aircraft flying low overhead. They switched off street lamps and told families to 'black-out' light from their windows, in case the glow helped guide German **bombers**. The government also helped families build air-raid shelters, and gave everyone gas masks.

These school children are practising wearing their gas masks.

Gas masks

These protected people from poison-gas attack. They had a rubber snout filled with cotton wool and charcoal, and a little window to see through. They were hot, smelly and clammy – and made rude noises when people wearing them tried to speak.

Gas mask for a baby.

Air-raid shelters

These protected people from bombs dropped by planes. Some were made of sandbags. Some were trenches dug into the ground. *Anderson shelters*, like this one built in gardens, were made of iron sheets covered with earth.

'We had long trenches made, each holding about 60 girls, with pumps to remove the nightly accumulation [collection] of water, and dim lighting from car batteries. ... on one occasion I remember being greeted by a cheer from each trench when I appeared with a barrowload of apple tart...'

A head teacher, from Chelmsford

'My schooldays were a terrible ordeal, carrying gas masks everywhere you went, sleeping in air raid shelters night after night...'

Betty, from Birmingham

Morrison shelters were strong metal cages that stood inside people's homes. Schools built their own special shelters, with room for all their pupils.

Mickey Mouse gas mask for young children 1939.

Children's gas masks often looked like favourite cartoon characters of the day. If you had to wear a gas-mask today, what character would you like your mask to look like?

Evacuation

Cities were dangerous in wartime. People living there were targets for enemy invaders and bombs. Many governments made plans to move children to safer places. This was called ‘evacuation’. Children were not forced to leave home, but parents were encouraged to send them away.

LEAVE THIS TO US SONNY—YOU OUGHT TO BE OUT OF LONDON

MINISTRY OF HEALTH EVACUATION SCHEME

British government poster, 1942.

Where did the children go?

Most children went to the countryside. They travelled without their parents on special buses or trains. Government organisers tied labels to their clothes, to show where they were going. At the end of their journey, they waited for foster parents to collect them and take them to new homes.

Children being collected by their new foster mother.

Some parents chose to send their children to friendly overseas countries. But in 1940, the British ship *SS City of Benares*, carrying 90 children to Canada, was sunk by a German submarine. Only 11 children survived. After this, few Britons risked sending their children abroad.

'The cow...has six sides, right, left, an upper and a below. At the back it has a tail, on which hangs a brush. With this it sends flies away...

Under the cow hangs the milk. It is arranged for milking. When people milk, the milk comes and there is never an end to the supply. How the cow does it I have not realised ....'

A cow, described by a city boy sent to the country.

Sad or happy?

Some children liked being sent away to safety. They thought it was an exciting adventure, and enjoyed seeing many new things. Others were unhappy because their foster parents were unkind, or because they missed their family and friends back home.

'She [our foster mother] used to bash the daylights out of the both of us...'

Maurice, from London

'This was another life – fresh country food, a room of my own...'

Bill, from Swansea

'The docks were full of people wanting to welcome us to Canada. A band was playing and people were throwing money onto the ship for us...we thought this was wonderful!'

Grace, sent to Canada

'This was such a happy time for me. I though I'd died and gone to heaven....'

Percy, sent to Canada

A new kind of War

World War 2 was different from all earlier wars. Armies on both sides tried to kill civilians (ordinary people), as well as enemy troops. Most civilians were killed by bombs dropped from aircraft, or in fires started by bombing raids.

St Paul's Cathedral, London, surrounded by flames after a German bombing raid in 1940.

Children sitting in the ruins of a bombed house.

In the Blitz

'Blitzkrieg' is a German word. It means 'lightning war'. It was also used by British people to describe massive German bombing raids on big cities in the early years of World War 2. (They shortened it to *'Blitz'*, which some people still use to mean 'smashed' today.) Between August 1940 and May 1941, 400 Londoners died, and 16,000 were injured in the Blitz. One Londoner in six was made homeless.

'Like other boys, I used to like exploring bomb sites, and hunting for shrapnel (bits of metal from bombs). Once I found a long sharp piece like a knife, about 30 cm long.'

Andrew, from Glasgow

Bomb deaths worldwide

About 60,000 British civilians were killed by German bombs. But Britain was not the only country to suffer in this way. Germany and Japan were bombed by the Allies, and over 400,000 Germans died. The world's worst bombing raid, on the city of Tokyo, Japan, killed 124,711 people. Many of the dead were children.

Londoners sheltered from the Blitz in underground railway tunnels.

My older sister and I carried my baby twin sisters...On the radio we heard with great horror the news: "Attention, a great air raid will come over our town...

Some minutes later we heard a horrible noise – the bombers. There were nonstop explosions....

We did not recognize our street any more. Fire, only fire wherever we looked. ... people, horses, all of them screaming and shouting in fear of death...

Lothar, from Dresden, Germany

The city of Dresden, Germany, was destroyed by bombs in 1943.

Divided families

All round the world, young men – and many young women – joined their national army, navy or air force to fight in the war. Their parents, wives, children, girlfriends and boyfriends were all left behind. Everyone tried to be brave and look cheerful when they said goodbye. But they all knew they might never see each other again.

Many children grew up with only people's memories of their father, and the letters their mothers had kept.

Unknown fathers

Many men were sent away to fight while their wives were pregnant. They waited anxiously, in army camps or on board warships, hoping to hear that their babies had been born safely, and that their wives were well. They longed to see their new-born sons or daughters and hold them in their arms.

Sadly, many fathers were killed before they could return home. So they never saw their babies at all. And many wartime babies grew up without knowing their fathers, who had died before, or soon after, they were born.

Saying goodbye.

"Junie, this happiness is nigh [almost] unbearable – a son! Darling, Junie! How did you do it? – I'm so proud of you, I'm beside myself – Oh you darling... Oh Junie, I wish I could be there – I think maybe I could be of some help – There are so many things to be done. What a ridiculous and worthless thing a war is in the light of such a wonderful event..."

Part of a letter written by an American airman to his wife when their son was born. He was killed fighting and never saw his baby.

Working mothers

Family life was broken up in other ways. Women worked long shifts in jobs that had been done by men before the war. They joined organisations like the Women's Voluntary Service, and ran first-aid posts or canteens (cheap cafes) to feed war-workers and people made homeless by bombs. They had little free time to spend with their children, and often felt exhausted.

Women worked for 12 hours or more every day, handling heavy machinery, sewing parachutes, packing ammunition or making bombs.

Children of the Holocaust

Jewish children on their way to safety.

In Nazi Germany from 1935, and German-ruled lands later on, Jewish people were not allowed to work, vote or marry non-Jews. They had to wear big yellow badges on their clothes. Jewish children were banned from schools.

The Holocaust

Six million Jewish people died in Hitler's camps – including 1.5 million children. Today, historians call this the '**Holocaust**'.

When the war began in 1939, many Jewish families tried to send their children away to safety. But this was very difficult. The Nazis would only let some children leave: those who had family overseas, or parents with money and connections to help them. About 10,000 went to live in Britain, Israel, Australia and the USA. But over a million were left behind.

The 'Final Solution'

In 1941, Nazi leader Adolf Hitler announced a horrible new plan. He called it 'the Final Solution'. Using this plan, Hitler aimed to kill all Jewish people. He sent them to terrible concentration camps (death camps), together with ethnic minority families, gay men, and people with disabilities. They were starved and tortured. Some died of disease; others were killed by poison gas. Very few survived.

Poem by Jewish girl

My heart still beats inside my breast
While friends depart for other worlds.
Perhaps it's better – who can say?
Than watching this, to die today?
No, no, my God, we want to live!
Not to watch our numbers melt away.
We want to have a better world.
We want to work – we must not die!'

Written by Eva Pickova, aged 12. She died in a German concentration camp.

Anne Frank, lived 1929-1945.

Jewish teenager Anne Frank and her family spent two years hiding from the Germans in the Netherlands (Holland). They were found and sent to a concentration camp, where Anne died, aged 16, in 1945.

While Anne Frank was hiding, she kept a diary, recording her hopes and fears. Here are a few extracts from her diary:

* 'I still believe, in spite of everything, that people are truly good at heart.'

* 'When I write, I can shake off all my cares.'

* 'I've reached the point where I hardly care whether I live or die.'

Children in prison

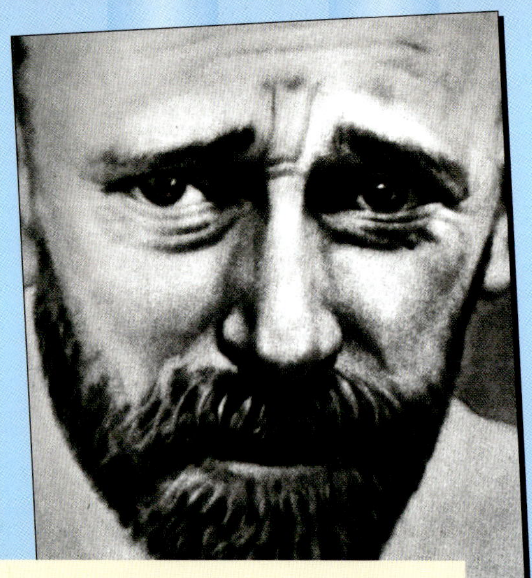

Janusz Korczak, a doctor who helped children in the Warsaw ghetto. He chose to be killed with them.

Before being sent to concentration camps, Jewish families were forced to live apart from other civilians. Some were crowded into city districts called 'ghettoes'. Others were shut away in big buildings, such as old army barracks or crumbling castles. Life there was like being in prison.

A normal life

Jewish parents tried to create a normal life for their children in prison. They taught lessons, sang songs, told stories, and played games. They helped children paint pictures and play music. These helped children express their anger, sadness – and fear.

This embroidered picture was made by a Jewish child in prison.

A lucky escape

In 1942, the Nazis ordered all boys and girls over 15 in one French prison to be moved to a concentration camp. About 40 teenagers were taken away. When the prison director heard about this, she bravely persuaded the Nazis to hand them back. Then she secretly helped them escape, to Switzerland and Spain.

This old castle was used as a prison for over 100 Jewish children.

Possible spies?

America also put children in prison during the war. They belonged to Japanese families living in the USA. The government did not trust Japanese-Americans. It thought they might work as spies for Japan. In prison, they were well-treated, but they were not free.

"Often I use to think as I laid on my pillow. What will happen to me if I have to live in this camp for five years?"

Part of a letter written by Louise Ogawa, a Japanese-American schoolgirl in an American army camp.

The 'War Effort'

Civilian men, women and children all wanted to help win the war. In Britain and America, governments asked them to 'make do and mend' – repair old clothes, shoes and furniture, instead of buying wasteful new ones. They told them to make tea from stinging nettles, keep pigs and chickens, and collect nuts and berries for food.

Children shared in all these tasks. They joined 'COGS' (clubs to collect rubbish), and 'dug for victory' by growing vegetables on school playing fields.

Collecting rubbish for recycling. Bones were used for explosives, paper for bullet cartridges, metal for aircraft – and hot water bottles for inflatable boats!

Government posters taught children to keep a lookout for spies. War stories helped them feel brave and proud.

Help from schools

Schools helped the war effort by collecting money to buy ships and planes, making clothes for fighting men, and joining in government savings schemes (lending money to the government), to help pay for the war. They sent gifts and cheering messages to troops a long way from home.

Schoolboys knitting woolly scarves for sailors.

Rationing

Food, clothes and fuel were all very scarce in wartime. It was too dangerous and expensive to import them from overseas. To make sure each person received enough to survive, governments set up **rationing** schemes. In Britain, everyone had a ration book, showing how much of the most important foods, such as meat or cheese, they were allowed to buy. Children got extra, nourishing foods, such as orange juice, but sweets, chocolate and bananas were rare luxuries. Most girls and boys wore second-hand clothes, and had very few toys.

An eager schoolboy using his first ration book.

Children join the fight

Most fighting men in World War 2 were between 18 and 40 years old. But some teenagers lied about their age, so they could fight earlier. There were also organisations that trained children from as young as 10 years old for war.

Children learn how to identify different aircraft shapes.

British boys joined the Air or Sea Scouts. They learned about ships and planes and practised drill (marching and obeying orders). Their sisters joined the Girls Training Corps. They learned first aid, drill, and signalling (sending messages using flags or sound signals known as Morse Code). In America, children joined High School Victory Corps and Junior Commando teams.

Joining up

'My brother quit high school to join the army. A lot of the boys did. ...Everybody was very patriotic [proud of their country] and they quit school to enlist [join].'

Eileen, from America

In Germany, children had to join the Hitler Youth aged 10. Girls learned nursing, childcare and housework. But boys were taught to fight fiercely, and given real guns. Some were sent into battle when they were only 12 years old.

Hitler youth

'You are our young team. You will take the storm flags from our hands and carry them to a better future. ...'

From a booklet given to all German boys and girls when they left school aged 14.

In the Resistance

Elsewhere in Europe, children joined Resistance movements – groups fighting Nazis who had invaded their country. They risked death by carrying messages hidden in their schoolbooks, or by helping Jewish people to escape.

Jeanne Agouau

French teenager Jeanne Agouau (above), helped lead two Jewish families over icy mountains in 1942

'We set out at 3am ... My father told everyone to keep as quiet as possible... The pace was slow. Everyone was tired... We had to go from rock to rock (they were climbing a rough path across mountains) while giving a helping hand to those who were exhausted... Jean Baptiste (later, Jeanne's husband) looked after the mother and grandmother... I carried the baby while leading the way to the frontier...'

Jeanne Agouau describes her brave, dangerous adventure.

The end of the War

Celebrating victory.

Happily reunited at last!

World War 2 ended in 1945, after Germany and Japan surrendered. People in Britain, America and the other Allied countries held joyful celebrations. They lit bonfires, let off fireworks, and danced all night in the streets. They held parties for everyone, from grandparents to young children. They decorated homes and shops with **bunting** and flags.

Sad memories

Everyone was pleased that the war was over. But many families also felt sad. They remembered their loved ones who had been killed in the fighting or in bombing raids.

Hard times

In many countries, civilians were still suffering. Their cities and communities had been destroyed by the war. They had no homes, few clothes, and hardly any food. Many thousands of children died from disease or starvation. Others had no parents to care for them, or had to flee from their homelands, as refugees.

There were also shortages in Britain and America. Food, clothes and fuel were rationed for several more years.

The Berlin Candy Bomber

After the war, American planes carried vital supplies of food and fuel to cold, hungry people in Germany. One kindly American pilot, Gail Halvorsen, also brought chocolate to cheer up German children. He made little parachutes out of handkerchiefs, tied the chocolate to them, and dropped them out of his plane over the German city of Berlin.

Children catching sweets dropped by the Berlin Candy Bomber.

Glossary

Allies – countries that were friends of the British

Axis powers – countries that were friends of the Germans

barrage balloons – balloons as big as cars, tied to very long, strong ropes

bombers – aircraft carrying bombs

bunting – coloured flags

candy – sweets and chocolate

Holocaust – an Ancient Greek word that originally meant 'burned sacrifice'. Later, it was used to mean 'immense destruction'. Today, it is most often used to describe the mass killing of Jewish people during World War 2

Nazi – A name given to a German political party

rationing – controlling supplies of food and other important goods, such as fuel, to make sure that everyone gets a fair share

USSR – Russia and the countries it controlled in east Europe and Asia

Index